Sarah

Goder bl

through .

God bless

Ron

God Help Me Grow

Learning to Pray through the Psalms

Ronald Oltmanns

For Titus and Markus and those young in the faith

Contents

Preface: Prayer

Prayer should be something that comes naturally to us. Like other important things it also needs to be learned.

Prayer is too important to leave to chance. We may feel we are not praying enough or very well. It's easy to wonder if it makes a difference at all.

Many wrong ideas and half-truths can arise, and if they aren't replaced with the full truth, our prayers shrink, they become selfish, and we don't pray often enough. Eventually we stop praying unless something is done about it.

This book is a training companion in prayer. It does not claim to be the only or best one available, but it will take you down the right path if you give your heart to this practice.

We will use the book of Psalms to train us in prayer. These prayers were first said over two thousand years ago and they have been used and turned to by God's people over many centuries. They effectively train us in the full language of prayer.

The psalms challenge our view of prayer, and that is good. They help us tell the truth about ourselves, both how we truly feel and who we really are. They keep us alert and in tune with what God is doing. They also train us to look deeper, listen closer and open our hearts wider so we can fully respond to God with all our heart.

Prayer is essential to life and fundamental to being human. Human beings have been praying over thousands of years and across every culture known even up to today. If that is news to you or you have not considered prayer essential to being human, it is time to lock on to that truth and begin practicing this elemental human act.

Prayer links us to God, who is the ultimate. Most curiously, God has been talking for a while and seeking to have a real conversation with us. The Psalms give critically important training in how to join that conversation and engage in it across a wider range of experiences, which is what God wants for us after all.

This book is a guide to using the Psalms to train us in prayer. It is not a commentary on the Psalms as literature or a textbook on theology. We aren't seeking to study the Psalms like we would in Bible study or to do a historical study of the long chain of psalm prayer among Jews and Christians.

One of the things the psalms teach us is to slow down and to let God's word speak to us. We do that through writing out our prayers, through repetition and through acts of worship. Take time to write, repeat the prayers, and to worship so you can get the real value from using this guide.

I started praying the Psalms over 20 years ago when I was living in Singapore. I did not have a guide or a lot of help in the process. People keep asking for that so I've written this guide to aid young believers in their spiritual growth. I hope it is a blessing to you, and I am looking forward to growing in the process too.

0 God

God—that's where I begin.
There's something in me that cries out to You,
especially when I'm scared, needing help or hurt.
That cry is prayer, and like any language, it is something
    I need to learn.
It takes practice, to listen to You, to lay it all out in the open
    before You.

God—You are where I'm going.
Even when I'm walking away, pointed in the wrong direction
My heart tells me so because You designed me that way.
Today I'm turning back to you again, pointing in the right
direction.
Your Spirit gives me grace to grow, so help me God.*

Get a journal or notebook you can write in. Write out your prayer to God. Write what's on your mind, what is in your heart that you want to bring to God. What question do you have? It may come quickly or immediately, but for many it takes a few minutes to come out. Wait for it to come.

As you write, point your thoughts and your heart to God.

If you have few words (or none at all) after waiting a while and listening, start by writing out the short prayer above. As you write, choose to make these words be your prayer to God.

When you are done (make sure you have written something), you have taken the first step. This is the beginning. I look forward to guiding you on this journey, but it is a path *you* have to walk.

Keep walking. We will talk some more to God tomorrow.

*In Hebrew, the personal name for God is YHWH and traditionally is not given vowels nor even pronounced. It is substituted by LORD, based on the traditional Jewish practice of reading "Adonai" (Lord) wherever YHWH is written. Scripture is clear that God has revealed Himself by name and wants to be known. Since this book is to help and encourage personal praying of the Psalms, I believe we can both maintain reverence and gain intimacy by using "Yahweh" as the personal, covenant name for God (Yahweh comes from filling in vowels for YHWH > YaHWeH). One place this is especially natural is when Yahweh is shortened to Yah, as in the word "HalleluYah" (Praise Yah!). I invite you to call on God by name as you pray and grow closer to Yahweh.

1 Derek

Do you know anyone named Derek? It's a good name; do you know what it means? If you're curious, you can go look it up. If you say *derek* you're also saying a word that sounds like a Hebrew word, an important word that features in Psalm 1. It's repeated three times. Can you guess which one?

1) Happy is one who does not walk by the advice of the wicked
Or stand around in the way of sinners, or sit with the mockers.
2) Instead, in the law ("torah"*) of Yahweh is his delight, and on
His law he meditates day and night.
3) He is like a tree planted beside canals filled with water which
produces fruit in the right season,
His leaves are lush, not withered, and everything he does prospers.
4) The wicked are not like this at all! They are like the stubble and
dry shells left after the good grain has been removed. That stuff is
thrown up in the air so the wind will carry it off, separating it from
the good grain.
5) The wicked will not be elevated ("rise up") in the judgment nor
sinners in the assembly of the righteous, 6) for Yahweh knows the
way of the righteous, but the way of the wicked will be wiped out.

The word *derek* in Hebrew is the word for "way, path" and in Psalm 1 it is in verse 1and twice in verse 6.

Two paths are pictured in this prayer, the path of the righteous and the way of the wicked. The wicked listen to the crowd, the rowdy ones who are bold about sin, who mock the way of the righteous and all things that point to God (beauty, truth, excellence). The happy path of the righteous focuses attention on God's law, listening to His words, meditating on them, repeating them over and over until they become part of him.

Look at the **results** of these two paths. The righteous tower like a healthy tree, well-watered and loaded with good fruit. The wicked are like hollow shells lacking substance, easily blown away by the wind. The **rewards** of each are also clear: when the test is given and results posted, the wicked won't pass. When the judge gives the final judgment, they will be condemned. The righteous will remain as a lasting group or assembly. They are known by the Lord and that gives security. They dedicate their lives to knowing God and his ways, his laws, and in the end they are known by Him.

Which way are you choosing?

Prayer: "God, I choose your way. I set my heart on You, tune my ears to Your voice, fix my eyes on Your laws. I will not listen to the crowd, or linger in the company of the wayward, or join in the jeers of the put-down masters and mockers. I will hide your word in my heart that I might not sin against You. Please give me fruit for my efforts, more fulfillment than I can imagine. I am choosing to be Yours today."

Find one verse from the Bible that inspires you to focus on God and the way of the righteous. Memorize it, write it down and call it to mind all day long. Need help choosing a verse? Why not Psalm 119:9 "How can a young person keep their path pure? By staying fixed on Your word."

Other Psalms like this: Psalm 5, 15, 19, 119

*Torah is the Hebrew word for law, teaching and is also used for the first five books of the Bible, the Law of Moses. Here it stands for the entire Teaching of God revealed to His people

2 Adore

Two things are most likely to keep you from praying. One is *wrong habits* or *bad choices*. Psalm 1 shows us we have to choose the right way, make the right choice over and over. When we delight in God's law, meditate on his word, have a habit of seeking Him each day, we have a good habit that will support us. When we listen to the wrong people over and over and hang out with them, it leads us down the path to destruction.

The other thing that will keep you from praying is belief. If you believe your prayers are not heard, or that God is small and the powers of this world are big, or that even if you pray nothing is going to happen, you won't continue praying for long.

With that warning in mind, we come to Psalm 2 and we pray it.

1) Why this hubbub among the nations, why this empty plotting by earth's people?
2) Rulers, kings and leaders of the earth are standing together against God and against His anointed king (*Mashiach,* Messiah*)
3) The bigshots say, "Let's break these bonds upon us, tear apart the cords wrapped around us.
4) The One seated in heaven laughs, Yahweh mocks them.
5) Then He speaks in His anger, and His burning words terrify them:
6) "I have set up *my* king on Zion, my holy mountain."

7) I will proclaim again Yahweh's decree. He said, "You are my son, today I have become your Father.
8) Just ask and the nations are yours, I will give you everything to the ends of the earth.

9) You will rule them in great strength with an iron rod, and break empires apart like they are clay jars."

10) "Kings, be wise (not foolish); rulers and leaders let yourself learn this lesson well:
11) Serve Yahweh with holy fear and tremble in His awesome presence.
12) Kiss the son (to show submission) or he will be angry and your way will be destroyed.
Happy and secure are all who take refuge in him."

The same word for "meditate" in Psalm 1:2 is used here in Psalm 2:1, but the nations are not meditating on God's Word. Instead they are focusing attention on their empty plans. We sometimes meditate on the wrong things! Worry is another kind of meditation that is faithless.

This psalm shows us that in a world full of bigshots, rich rulers, and important things happening all around, all of these things are laughed at by a God who is truly Big and awesomely powerful. Our prayers are heard by the King of Heaven, so we should pray boldly.

God's Messiah is ruling and all leaders, kings and powers will bow before Him. The right attitude is to adore the true King and His anointed, the Messiah. Psalm 1 told us you'll be happy if you choose the right way (meditate on God's Word). Psalm 2 ends by telling us we'll be happy if we submit to God and take refuge in Him.

Pray: Where do you need to submit to God?
What do you need to trust God for?
Turn your heart to Him in worship and adoration. Write out your prayer to Him today.

Other Psalms like this: 89, 46, 18

3 OMG

Some people may not like the reference to "Oh my God", but even if the words are casually thrown around too often, they point us in the right direction.

Prayer is not limited to pretty church buildings or to people who mouth pretty words. Prayer is actually available now if you just call on God. "Yahweh!" "O God!"

Psalm 3 reminds us of David and his desperate situation when one of his sons (Absalom) tried to take his kingdom away from him.

Not knowing exactly what to say or how to say it with poetic words that sounded good, his prayer went something like this: "O my God! I'm surrounded by people who oppose me. I'm surrounded by people, enemies everywhere, people planting doubts and denying You will help me at all. It's overwhelming and discouraging! But God, you are my protection, my shield and I cry out to You, looking to You alone for answers. I won't worry or toss and turn through sleepless nights. I trust in You. Even ten thousands of people will not frighten me. Rise up and deliver me God! Deliverance is in You, blessing is in You. Amen"

Read the words to Psalm 3 at least twice today. It will change your praying.

1) Yahweh, how many are my enemies! So many rise up against me.
2) Many are saying to me, 'God won't help you.'
3) But God, you are a shield around me, my glory and the One who lifts my head.
4) I cry out loudly to Yahweh and He answers me from his holy mountain.

5) I lay down and sleep; I wake up again for Yahweh keeps me going.

6) I am not afraid of ten thousands of people who are set against me on all sides.

7) Rise up Yahweh! Save me my God!

8) Slap the face of my enemies, knock out the teeth of the wicked [so they will stop pressing me].

9) Saving help comes from Yahweh, Your blessing be on Your people.

OMG is not said with giggles or in mock surprise. It is a powerful, potent prayer when we turn our hearts to God. Even against impossible odds, in overwhelming situations, God is there for us. That is good news! You don't need magical words or beautiful words to get God's attention. Speak the truth from your heart and call on Him.

Prayer: Who are you trusting? Turn your prayer to God and use whatever words come from deep in your heart. Write it in your journal.

Other Psalms like this: 5, 7, 9, 13, 31, 39, 71, 77, 88

4 Good Night

If your parents were (or are) religious, they probably taught you to say your prayers at night. Nighttime is a good time to pray, to talk to God and open up your heart to Him.

If you have never developed this habit, or if you are out of practice, it's not too late to start.

Is there anything bothering you? Are you happy about something that happened today? How are you feeling about tomorrow and what is likely to meet you in the morning? Any of this (or all of it) can be brought to God in an evening prayer.

1) Answer me when I call, faithful [righteous] God
You cleared away my trouble; be merciful to me and listen to my prayer ("tephilah"*).
2) How long will others mock my glory?
How long will they love empty lies and seek falsehoods?
3) Know that Yahweh sets apart the faithful for Himself;
Yahweh hears when I call to Him.
4) Tremble and shake with your agitation and anger, yet sin no more;
Reflect in your hearts as you lie on your bed and keep silent
5) Offer worthy worship and trust in Yahweh.
6) Many say, "Who will show us some blessing?"
Lift up the light of your favor Yahweh [that we may be blessed by Your presence].
7) *You* fill my heart with more joy than they have when their grain and wine multiply.
8) In peace I lie down and sleep sound, for it is You Yahweh who gives me true security.

The key in this prayer is where we put our focus, our attention. We can be aware of our troubles, the mocking of others, their bad choices and how they stir up my anger and frustration. All of these have room for expression in this prayer. But they don't steal attention away from where it belongs. *God* is the one who deserves the focus, my attention, my prayer and trust.

God works in me to calm me and bring me peace when I call on Him, when I silence myself before Him. It's not God's blessings and the good things of life that satisfy. What brings real joy is God's presence, God Himself. Peace, security, joy, favor—these are all in God.

This is a prayer I can pray!

Read through the psalm again, slowly and make the words your own. Take them into your heart and let them soak in. Say this prayer at night and sleep sound in God.

Other Psalms like this: 11, 17, 63, 23, 27, 30, 91, 121

Tephilah is "prayer" in Hebrew and comes from the word for arguing a legal case or speaking up for someone.

5 Morning Prayer

We wake up in the morning after we said our prayers and went to bed. What has been going on? We have been sleeping (unless your had a difficult sleepless night). Maybe you had a dream. But God was not sleeping. God continues to do His work even while we sleep. On the other side of the world there were also people awake and working.

So what do you do as you rise from bed? Get something to eat? Turn on the tv or radio or check your mobile device? Rouse others and get the day started? Or do you pray?

Psalm 5 leads us in how to get the rhythms of the day started right.

1) Listen to my words Yahweh, decipher my murmuring (muttering)*.
2) Hear my cry for help, my king and my God, because I'm praying to *You*.
3) O Yahweh, hear my voice at dawn; at dawn I set it all out before you and look out for your answer.
4) You are not a God who delights in wickedness, *You* offer no welcome of any kind to evil.
5) The boastful cannot stand before you; you hate all who practice evil.
6) You destroy those who speak lies; Yahweh you cast off in disgust traitors who deceive.
7) However, it's by the abundance of your faithful love I enter your house.
    I bow down at your holy temple in fear and awe.
8) O Yahweh, lead me in your righteous (path); because of my watchful enemies , line out your way (derek) before me.
9) For nothing they say can be relied on; their ruin is near.
    Their throat is an open grave, their tongues drip flattery.
10) Condemn them, O God, make them fall by their own tricks.

Cast them out for their many sins, for they rebel against *You*.

11) But all those who take refuge in You are glad,
They are ever giving a shout of praise as You cover them.
Let those who love Your name rejoice in You.

12) For *You* Yahweh bless the righteous; your great big shield of
favor surrounds them.

There is an echo here of Psalm 1, the two ways (*derek*, remember?) of the righteous and the wicked.

But notice how the attention is given to God throughout. The focus keeps returning back to God. Just when we are about to get distracted by all of our busy activity, or caught up in how bad people can be, the prayer keeps calling out to God, calling Him by name, fixing our heart back on Him.

What is *your* heart cry to God this morning? What do you want to say to Him, the Ruler and King who never sleeps, the great Shield whose favor covers us? Write it out now.

Other Psalms like this: Psalm 30, 90, 143

*Murmuring-*hagigi,* the word itself in Hebrew sounds like a muttering or low murmured sound that is barely understandable.

6 Distress

You have landed in trouble. It's not a small problem, it is intense and you know it is serious.

When that happens, we're tempted to point to others. "Look at them! What they are doing is wrong!" It may be. We don't have to look far to see people left and right who are doing wrong, who are making the situation worse, not better.

But other people aren't the problem. The problem is me.

1) Yahweh, do not rebuke me in your anger, do not chastise me in your hot rage.
2) Show me favor, Yahweh, for I am frail. Yahweh, heal me for I sit in terror down to my bones.
3) My soul suffers in the extreme, and You, Yahweh—O, how long?!

4) Turn Yahweh, rescue me! Save me because of your steadfast love.
5) No one remembers You in death and in Sheol* who knows You?
6) I grow weary from my groaning, every night my bed is flooded with my tears, my couch is soaked through!
7) My eyes are clouded and swollen with grief, worn out from all who harass me.
8) Away from me all you who stir up trouble, for Yahweh hears my weeping!

9) Listen Yahweh to my pleading, O Yahweh accept my prayer.
10) All my enemies will be ashamed and struck with great terror, They will turn back and suddenly be struck with shame.

When we are in distress, we should take time to look: Are we separated from God because of our sin? Have we dealt with the problem at our core, have we given God control of our life?

If so, we can deal with the rest because we have God's help on our side. If not, no matter what we do, we will feel frustrated and ultimately distressed. It is a warning signal that sin has separated us from God.

Prayer: look inside yourself, and invite God to do the same. Is there any sin you need to face? Is your situation made worse by people around you who are frustrating and opposing you? Ask for God's help in dealing with them. Write out your prayer to God in your journal. Write the words to Psalm 6:4,9

Other Psalms like this: Psalm 32, 38, 51, 77, 130, 143

Sheol – "the underworld", in the Hebrew worldview it is where people rest in death, but not equal to Hell

7 Righteous God

Even if we have chosen the *derek* or path of righteous living, meditating on God's law daily, we have to deal with others who have not made that choice. We know from Psalm 2 about the kings and rulers who dare to oppose God and His Messiah and are brought down to humble submission.

But what about those who oppose the righteous, who do wrong without being provoked? What about the people who attack *me* when I didn't do anything wrong?

Psalm 7 directs our questions, our pleading and our sense of unfairness to God. Don't take matters in your own hands or seek revenge. Let *God* deal with them. Draw even closer to God and trust Him to deliver you. This is something you can count on God to do.

1) O Yahweh, my God! In you I seek refuge. Save me from all my pursuers—deliver me!
2) If you don't, just like lions they will tear me to pieces, dragged off with no one to search for or deliver me.
3) O Yahweh, my God, *if* I have really done such awful things, if there is such violent guilt on my hands,
4) *If* I have backstabbed my friends or given aid to my attacker without good reason
5) Let the enemy pursue and overtake me, let them stomp me to pieces in the ground, let my "glorious lies" lay there in the dust.

6) Rise, O Yahweh, in your holy anger, rise against my raging enemies. Rouse Yourself O God and give judgment. 7) The nations are gathered for the hearing and you are seated on the high throne. 8) Yahweh judge the peoples. Judge *me* Yahweh in line with my righteousness and innocence.

9) Avenge and halt the evil of the wicked; uphold and protect the righteous.

You thoroughly examine the mind and heart O righteous God!

10) My shield is God Himself. He delivers the upright heart.

11) God judges the righteous and approves them; and there is no mistake ever in His judgments.

12) If the wicked does not turn away from sharpening his sword and setting his bow, 13) making flaming arrows and preparing deadly weapons...

14) Watch out! The birth pains have come on strong—something evil is about to be born! He conceived [got pregnant with] his own harm and trouble and now he's having the baby; the lie has become a life of its own and it's just going to keep growing!

15) He dug a pit, a deadfall trap for others to fall into. 16) Go back and you'll see his mischief has backfired and the violence he planned has all come down on his own head.

17) I praise Yahweh for his righteousness, I'm singing praise to Yahweh Most High!

In this prayer there is a clear, strong sense that right and wrong will not get confused. God will make the distinction, and right will be rewarded. Wrong and evil—no matter how well-planned, clever or threatening—will be wiped out by God who sees that justice is surely done in the end.

The pictures of righteousness and wickedness—and their consequences—are very vivid. The celebration is not glee at the torture of my enemies, but sincere praise to a Righteous God.

Prayer: Do you have anyone giving you trouble now? Bring it to God who is righteous and trust Him to take care of it. If no one is giving you trouble or trying to do you harm, give thanks to God and pray that

He fills you with His righteousness so you can pray verses 3-5, 8 and 10 with all sincerity. Write out your prayer in your journal.

If you are the one who has been doing wrong return to Psalm 6 from yesterday and pray it again.

Other Psalms like this: 44, 94, 50, 71

8 Majestic

Prayer in the Bible seems to move in two ways. One is crying out for help and the other is lifting up praise. The two can go together in the same prayer as many of the Psalms show us.

Which do you do more often? Do you ask God for what you need (or maybe it's what you *want*), or do you spend time praising, thanking and trying to honor God?

Psalm 8 sings out God's glory, and even in the strangely exalted position humans seem to have in God's creation, the fact remains that it is *God* who set things up this way.

1) Yahweh, our Lord, how majestic and magnificent* is Your name all over the earth!
Let Your splendor be displayed across the heavens 2) and pour from the mouths of children and infants.
You are secure from all challengers and You easily dispatch hostile and determined enemies.

3) When I gaze on Your heavens, what you have fashioned with Your fingers, the moon and stars that You set in their places...
4) What are humans that you even notice them at all? Why have any concern about mankind 5) that You make people just a little less than heavenly beings, that You give them glory and majesty [like a king who gives a crown to his heir]?
6) You made him ruler over all things You made in this world, You put everything under his feet:
7) all sheep and cattle and the wild animals too, 8) the birds and the fish and everything else in the sea.

9) Yahweh, our Lord, how majestic and magnificent* is Your name all over the earth!

The main point or theme of this prayer is stated at the beginning and repeated at the end, just in case you might miss it.

Praise God for His majesty, might, His magnificence in everything He has made. He has made us to comprehend this, to celebrate it and to rule over His creation for His glory.

Prayer: God, I don't understand Your ways or Your power, but my mind and my heart bow down before You to worship You for who You are. Lift up my mind and my heart to rule, to take charge of the creation around me and to take care of it, to create and to live in it each day more fully aware of Your presence. Show me Your ways and give me power to walk in them.

Write your own five lines of praise to God today in your journal.

Other Psalms like this: Psalm 19, 95, 104, 148

*vv. 1,9 *magnificent (ad'ir)* "mighty, magnificent, majestic" – this anchors the theme of the whole psalm, beginning and end: the majesty and excellence of God.

9 Justice

Read all of Psalm 9 in your Bible.

Do you notice something new? Do you see some familiar themes too?

What is new is the note of joy, the praise and thanksgiving and the heartfelt delight in God at the beginning. In Psalm 5 there a brief burst of joy at the end as part of the morning prayer. Here it is loud and bold, right up front.

What is familiar? Do you notice the enemies or God's righteous judgment? What about the verse (v. 15) that echoes Psalm 7? As we continue praying with the Psalms, you should start to see or notice some themes like these and others emerge.

Take a minute to meditate on the following verses from this psalm:
1) I praise Yahweh with all my heart, I declare all Your miraculous deeds.
2) I delight and rejoice in You, I sing songs of praise to Your name Most High [One].

7) Yahweh abides forever; He has set up his throne for judgment
8) He will judge the world in righteousness, He rules the peoples with fairness/uprightness.
9) Yahweh is a refuge for the oppressed, a refuge during the drought (lack of rain).
10) Those who know Your Name trust You, for You Yahweh will not abandon those who seek You.

Prayer:
God, how do I pray this prayer? How do I sing this song?
How do I claim Your cover from those who would do me wrong?

I am not righteous in my own right. I belong to people You have blessed.

King, You reign in right. Yah, You rule with justice. You give refuge to the pressed, trust is truly rewarded in You.

Sing this praise in Zion! Take this news out to the nations, God does not ignore or forget our cries.

(add lines of your own)

Other Psalms like this: Psalm 27, 34, 65, 94, 95

10 Pride

Pride is supposed to be a good thing, right? When you are proud of your country, your family or where you are from, there's nothing wrong with that.

What about when someone does wrong and they are proud of that? When someone uses their strength and sneakiness to win, get rich, trample on people and they are proud of this, something is not right. When they are so proud that they mock God and think their place will never be shaken and that God is weak, absent, or unconcerned—watch out!

Read all of Psalm 10 in your Bible.

Go back and think about (meditate) on these verses from the psalm, using them to begin your prayer to God.

1) Why, Yahweh, do You keep Your distance? Why are You hidden when times are so bad?
2) The wicked in their pride are bearing down on the poor—let *them* be caught in their own evil schemes.
3) For the wicked boasts of his runaway appetite for evil, and his whole life is about making a buck while "blessing" (actually cursing) Yahweh with disrespect.
4) The wicked with his nose in the air snorts, "There's no God seeking out justice", and there is no place for God in all his thoughts/plans.
5) His ways (derek)seem to prosper all the time; Your judgments on high are out of sight and out of mind, and he blasts away his enemies.
6) He assures himself, "I will not be shaken, I will never ever meet with trouble or any obstacle."

7) His mouth is full of cursing, fraud, and violence, and he has plenty more in store, ready to cause trouble and bring disaster.

12) Rise up, Yahweh! Take action and show You have not forgotten the lowly and afflicted.
13) Why should the wicked get away with mocking You God, thinking to himself "You don't root out evil"?
14) You *do* see. You fully notice every harm, every grief, and You take charge of setting things right,
The wronged and bullied can entrust themselves to You and You help the orphans and most vulnerable.

16) Yahweh is king forever and always; the nations perish from his land.
17) Yahweh, You listen to the longings of the weak, the poor and afflicted, You will strengthen their hearts and tune Your ears to them, 18) to judge rightly for the orphan and the distressed and put a stop to the bullying ways of these boastful brutes.

This psalm is somewhat the opposite of Psalm 1; things are reversed. Here the righteous are suffering and the wicked seem to be prospering and flaunting their evil, proud of getting everything *their* way (certainly not Yahweh's way).

Who are you most like: the proud, the lowly, or the one watching all this happen? Pray that God will speak to your heart and help you to do the right thing in your situation. This calls for real prayer, a cry to God to set things right, to judge and put right and wrong back in place. Make this your prayer today.

Prayer: God, help me grow by seeing pride and arrogance in myself and others. God, come to the rescue of those who are bullied by the proud. Let your power be shown and put things right. It's not right for the wicked to prosper, to stomp on people or to mock You. You are King, and You care for the poor. Give me a heart that cares for the discouraged and those that the proud prey on. Amen

Other Psalms like this: Psalm 14, 55, 35, 37, 73, 94, 79

11 Trust

Where do you go when life gets rough? Imagine true danger entering the picture for a minute. What if you had an advance warning that someone wanted to beat you up? Or bad weather like a hurricane, tornado, tsunami or blizzard was headed for your home? What would you do then?

The natural reaction is to flee, to get away from danger. People around you will tell you the same thing. "Get out of here! Lay low for a while until you are out of danger."

If you are in danger, where are you going to go? Places that seem safe may not really be so. If you feel threatened, give careful thought to where you turn and look for help. Now read through Psalm 11.

1) In Yahweh I seek refuge; how can you say to me, "Flee to the mountains, bird"?
2) Look! The wicked bend the bow, the arrow is on the string, ready to shoot under the cover of dark at the upright in heart.
3) The foundation is destroyed, so what are the righteous to do?
4) Holy is Yahweh in his temple. Yahweh reigns from His throne in the heavens.
  In the flash of an eye He examines all of mankind
5) Yahweh examines the righteous, but the wicked who love violence He hates.
6) He will rain down on the wicked—get this—bird-trapping snares that are made of fiery sulphur; raging winds that scorch will be what *they* get as a reward.
7) For Yahweh is righteous; He loves righteous deeds. The righteous will see His face!

This psalm doesn't just urge us "Trust God." It says it in a much more colorful way. The question we started with is still there: "When danger comes, if you have time to react what are you going to do?" The one praying gets advice to get out of town, run to the mountains. In fact, "*fly* to the mountains, bird!" It's not just danger you are facing, but really sneaky attack (they're shooting in the dark when you can't see what's coming). Listen to the reason given: it's all gone down the drain, and what chance do the righteous have anyway?

But this pray-er is not listening to common wisdom or sensible advice. He is fleeing to Yahweh whose holiness is greater than the wickedness of evil men. Yahweh reigns in heaven, high above the temporary safety that a mountain seems to provide.

Yahweh will entrap these evil "birds" in a snare of fire. If you are fleeing from danger, the only safe place to be is in the hands of holy, righteous Yahweh.

Prayer: What area or situation in your life needs you to show trust in God? Make a point of trusting more fully in God as you pray this psalm again. At the end, finish this prayer. "God, I'm trusting You in _____. Show Your righteousness in _____ and show me Your face."

Other Psalms like this: Psalm 121, 62, 91

12 Even When

What do you do when things around you are bad, bleak and hopeless? Not just bad for you, but bad everywhere.

Have you heard people around complaining about how bad things have gotten? How do you pray at *those* times?

Psalm 12 gives us some guidance for praying *even when* everything seems hopeless and no one has any desire for godliness.

1) Deliver, Yahweh, for the godly are no more, the faithful have vanished from humanity!
2) Everyone tells his neighbor empty things; they speak with false lips and a double heart.
3) Yahweh will cut off all false and flattering lips, He'll put an end to all big talk.
4) They claim, "It's what we say* that makes things happen. With *our own* lips we will rule! Who else is going to rule us?"

5) "The oppression of the weak and poor, the distressful cry of the needy—enough! Now I will arise," says Yahweh, "I will make them safe from those who rage against them."
6) What *Yahweh* says is a true saying, like a promise you can bank on.
Its truth is pure like refined silver, super-refined seven times in a great earthen furnace.
7) Yahweh, You will protect us from danger and guard us forever from this faithless age 8) even when vile things are valued by humanity and the wicked prowl all around.

Evil and darkness have always gone together with untruth, lies and falseness. In this prayer the false lips and empty talk of mankind, the broken promises and unfaithfulness of all sinful people is first silenced by God (v. 3).

Those who are bullied and beat down get heard. God will rescue them. Finally, in contrast to the falseness, lies and empty talk of the wicked (which God will silence), God's speech, His words and what He promises is pure, priceless and full of truth that carries weight. In an elaborate illustration, what God says is compared to silver that has passed through seven stages of purification, making it unmatched in its genuine purity.

Most of the psalms end on this note of confident trust in God or in lifting up God's way as the final word. This prayer states the truth about God but then does something a little different, acknowledging the messiness that is still there.

Right now, we're still living among the muck and confusion and wickedness—all of which make it even more important to pray and cry out to God in faith, to hold to His lasting truth instead of surrendering to the conspiracy of evil and lies. What is the truth you need to embrace (God will rescue, God hears me, Good will triumph, etc.)? What is the lie you need to deny (Evil does not pay, Lies do not make things better, Darkness will not triumph)?

Prayer: God, You are truth and what You say is really so. I will not be discouraged or defeated by falsehood. Even when evil surrounds, I will trust in You, especially in _____(fill in with the truth you need to embrace and the lie you will deny)_. Amen.

Other Psalms like this: Psalm 88, 55, 140

say v. 4 (Heb. literally has "tongue") The mention of lips and tongue emphasizes that the ungodly rely on the power of what they say.

13 How Long?

Have you ever been waiting on someone to meet you or pick you up and the waiting got a little long? "Did they forget about me?" you wonder.

It is hard to deal with these waiting times. If you can't move on and do something you just feel worse. Your mind might even make things up, "Why are they doing this to me?"

There are situations even worse than that where we can feel trapped. Is God letting me suffer? I can't stand this any longer!

If you turn to God in prayer, you may feel like complaining loudly, "How long? God, what is taking so much time?" Our prayer today is exactly like that.

1) How long* Yahweh will You forget me—forever? How long will You conceal Your face from me?
2) How long must I hold advice within and not act, experience grief in my heart by day?
How long will my enemy stay on top of me?
3) Consider this carefully and answer me Yahweh my God! Give me some light through all this darkness, or I will go to sleep in death 4) and the enemy will gloat, "I've won", rejoicing that I have been tripped up and taken down.

5) Yet I trust in Your faithful love, my heart rejoices in Your deliverance. I sing praise to You Yahweh for You have done good to me.

Waiting can be hard. The darkness can be so great that we suspect we will die before an answer comes. To be pinned down under the enemy—that's impossible to endure!

Yet...the darkness cannot extinguish all hope, and the tiniest seed of faith—as small as a mustard seed—can still take root and grow into rejoicing and praise. In fact, trust and praise and rejoicing are the most effective answer to the question, "How long?" As long as it takes, God, I'm going to praise You in the meantime. And when Your deliverance comes I will rejoice and praise You more.

Have you been waiting for something for a long time? Bring it to God in prayer today.

Prayer: Lord, sometimes I have to wonder "how long" before You set it all right, how long before my prayer is answered? Be with me as I wait and trust. Be with me especially in _____, which seems dark and hopeless, where defeat is more real than victory. Consider it carefully Lord and send some light into this darkness today. Shine Your light within me. Amen

Ad nah? - "How long?" is repeated four times in the first two verses. Sometimes, we can only manage to pray *Ad nah, Yahweh?* How long, my God?

Other Psalms like this: Psalm 42-43, 31, 77

14 Evil Everywhere

It is a spiritual truth that God is everywhere. However, not only are there people who deny it, they can point out places where God seems absent. On a practical level, there's no god stopping them from doing whatever they please, at least for now. But not forever.

Today's prayer doesn't just repeat, "God is everywhere" and ignore those who say otherwise. It tackles the problem forcefully and calls God-deniers "fools" and shows where that path leads. It also shows us the only way forward: seeking God with insight and understanding, being wise and calling on God to save.

1) A fool thinks to himself, "There is no God."
They are corrupted, ruined, they act horribly, no one does good.
2) Yahweh looks down from heaven on humanity to see if there is anyone with insight and understanding. Do any really seek God?
3) All have turned aside from God and joined together in "going bad." No one does good—not a single one!
4) Do they really not know, all of them doing evil by devouring my people? They eat Yahweh's bread but don't call on Him.
5) There they shake, trembling in fear, for God is found among the righteous.
6) The plans of the poor may be put down, because *Yahweh* is their final refuge (not their plans).
7) Who will bring salvation for Israel out of Zion? Yahweh will bring back his captive people, and Jacob will shout and Israel will rejoice.

This psalm has strong connections with Psalm 10, and in Hebrew Psalm 10:4 "there is no God" is worded the same at 14:1 "There is no God". This is a denial of God's presence. But denying God is very arrogant. To do that is to put yourself on a godlike level and claim you know all the truth and have evidence necessary to deny God. This psalm calls that foolish and corrupted.

In fact, evil and wickedness *are* destructive and negative. But if there is no God, how do we explain good and evil? How do we explain purposeful creation? We can see every day that it is easier to tear things down than it is to build them up.

God looks down for those wise enough to seek Him. What God is masterful at is creating, making things good, restoring, healing, constructive work. The righteous and wise are lining up with God in building something positive: restoration, salvation, celebration.

The world we live in looks like evil is everywhere. Look closer, though, and you will see God at work among the righteous. The bigger reality is that there is more than just the world we live in. There is a God in heaven and His expert work is in setting things right, which includes salvation even for this world.

Prayer: God, open our eyes to see more of what you see, more than the evil and corrupt and tiresome things all around us. Open our hearts to know You more, to seek You and to set our hearts on the things You care about. You are our refuge. You live among the righteous. Save and deliver me from _____. Let all tremble before You—there is a living God among us!

Other Psalms like this: Psalm 53

15 Who?

Often in prayer, we come to God with requests for what we want. Sometimes we have questions. And sometimes we get a full, detailed answer to our questions like we do in Psalm 15. Read it over slowly and let it soak in.

1) Yahweh, who may camp in your tent*? Who may live on your holy mountain?
2) The one who lives in integrity, practices righteous living and speaks the truth in his heart,
3) The one who does not slander others, who does no harm to his friend, and does not taunt or provoke his neighbor,
4) The one who despises what is hateful yet honors those who fear* Yahweh, who does not change what he swore even when it works against him,
5) Who has not collected interest on his money nor accepted a bribe that harms the innocent—the one who lives this way will never be shaken.

Who does God welcome into His presence? What kind of person is God looking for? We get an eleven point answer that emphasizes the heart, the attitude and habits of the person God wants us to be.

This is an extended version of Psalm 1 that introduced us to the righteous person who chooses the right way (derek). This psalm is not a list of what "qualifies" you to enter God's presence. Instead, we get a description of the kind of person God wants to shape us into if we desire to spend our lives with Him.

As you go back to the psalm and pray through it again, make it your prayer after each item: "Yes God, make me into this kind of person." Is there one or maybe two specific areas where God is wanting to shape you? Write that down in your journal. Ask God to show you more specific ways you can become the person who enjoys God's presence.

Other Psalms like this: Psalm 27, 24

*v. 1 tent...holy mountain – these probably refer to the holy Tent of Meeting where the Ark of the Covenant was kept (see Exodus 25:8-22) and the Mt. Zion where people went to worship God. The important idea here is these places represent the presence of God where men can approach Him.

*v. 4 fear Yahweh (*yirah Yahweh*) – fear of God means we honor, respect, and revere Him. It is a key truth taught in Proverbs and in the Wisdom books of the Bible (the fear of God is the beginning of wisdom)

16 Delight

Take a minute to think of a time when you felt fantastic. How long did it last? How would you describe it in words? Do you know what caused it?

When we pray sometimes God can seem very far off, and there are psalms (such as laments) that help us pray in those moments. Psalm 16 leads us into a close and personal experience of prayer to God.

1) Guard me, God, for in You I take refuge.
2) I say to Yahweh, "*You* are my Lord, there is nothing better for me than You."
3-4) The "holy and mighty ones" in the land* are like second or third wives that people get in place of You, the First Love. My great wish for those who get another god is that You increase their worries and troubles. I will not join in pouring out bloody offerings or repeat their names with my lips.
5) You Yahweh are all I have and stand to gain. *You* have hold of my future.
6) A beautiful inheritance has been marked out for me, what a pleasing set of gifts You have in store!
7) I bless Yahweh who counsels and guides me, and at night He corrects and trains my sense of right and wrong.
8) I keep Yahweh in mind, always present before me so I will never stumble or be shaken.
9) So my heart rejoices, my whole being jumps for joy, even while my body rests secure,
10) Sure that You will not forget me and leave me in Sheol* or let Your faithful servant be put in the Pit (grave).
11) You will show me the path that leads to life. In Your presence is joyful delight, You give pleasure that never ends.

How do we pray this kind of prayer if we are not feeling a strong or intense affection for God?

It starts with being aware of *danger*. There are many things to distract us from God. There are people who compete with God for our attention and affection. We don't see this as dangerous for our soul, but it is. This prayer shakes us fully awake and calls out for God to guard and provide refuge for us.

Next, we *surrender* to God. All our toys and treats and all our goods—we give them up and confess, "*You* are my Lord, there is nothing better for me than You."

We must also turn away from other gods. Don't be too quick to deny that there are other "gods" in your life. What has the appearance of holiness, the rumble of awesomeness, the mighty power that seems so cool, but does not draw you closer to the true God? Turn away from false gods.

You are like a cup, beautifully made by God. But over time you have let things inside that are not healthy or clean or holy. This is the danger you face. The surrender and turning away is like pouring that stuff out of your cup.

But God doesn't leave you there with an empty cup! Now He can fill you up with the good stuff. The best thing of all is more of God—His love and grace and holiness and everything that is truly good.

God has a future and a purpose for you. He wishes to guide and counsel you. And He will not stop short of the goal, even when you die. That could come much later in your life or sooner than you think. God will show you the path that leads to life which leads into His presence and intense, joyful delight that never ends.

Prayer: Now go back and pray this prayer while letting God work its truth deep into your heart. What a delight you are in for! Enjoy all the fullness God wants to give you.

Write in your journal today's date and make a note of what you prayed and where you are putting your hope for today and for the rest of your life. You can find real delight and pleasure in reading this again later.

Other Psalms like this: Psalm 23, 27, 28, 63, 91

*vv. 3-4 *The "holy and mighty ones" in the land*...there is more than one way to translate these verses. One very popular way of translating into English is "As for the saints in the land in whom I delight". The translation here points to false gods and brings the thought of vv. 3-4 together; it best fits the overall theme of the psalm.

*v. 10 *Sheol* – "the underworld", in the Hebrew worldview it is where people rest in death, but not equal to Hell. We read this first in Psalm 6 and will see it again in other psalms.

17 Are You Listening?

Sometimes we can't help but wonder, "Does God really hear us? Are my prayers really heard?"

Psalm 17 gives us specific words for these concerns, and it does it in three different ways.

First, we call on God to hear. This prayer shows us we can *boldly* call on God.

1) Hear, righteous Yahweh, pay attention to my cry of lament, listen with favor to my prayer spoken without falsehood.
6) I call on You, and You will answer me God. Turn your ear to me and hear what I'm saying.

That's five times that God is called on to hear, to listen, to attend to the prayer going up. The first way this psalm helps us to pray is it urges us: call on God, press your case with Him, have confidence that He listens.

Second, in answer to the question, "Does God really hear us?" we get this answer: not only does He hear us, but *He comes to see us.*

2) Let my verdict come from Your presence, and let your eyes see with integrity.
3) You have visited me at night and examined my heart ; you refined me and found no evil plans, nothing that dishonors You coming out of my mouth.
15) I will see Your face because I'm righteous, I am satisfied with what I have seen of You when I have woken up.

This prayer reminds us of Psalms 3-5 that all mention praying at night and finding an answer in the morning. Not only does God hear in heaven, He visits us at night, we see Him upon waking. God comes to see us and blesses us with His presence.

Finally, when we have doubt or questions about God hearing, listening or caring about our prayers, there is this word for us: know with certainty and expect God to hear.

6) I call on You, and You will answer me God.
7) Show Your faithful love* in wonders O Saver of those who seek refuge from their enemies in Your strong right hand.
8) Protect me as You would guard the pupils of Your own eyes*; hide me in the shadow of Your wings.

These are words of great tenderness and intimacy that describe how God takes care of us.   We are precious in His eyes; He will hide us under His protective wing.   These words show us we can pray in expectation and certainty that He cares and will answer.

Prayer: God, You hear me. Yahweh, You see me and will come to visit me with Your presence. You hold me close in Your protection and will not ignore my prayer.   Here is what I bring from my heart to You today _____.   Thank You!

*v. 7 "Faithful love" (*chesed*) is a Hebrew word best translated in English as "faithful love" or "steadfast love". It shows God's covenant-keeping nature and His constancy in loving us.   We first saw this in Psalm 5:7 and will encounter it against throughout the Psalms (see Psalms 136, 119, 86:13, 25:7, 51:1, 103:8, 89:2 and many other places).   Older translations sometimes used "tender mercies" to translate this.   God's *chesed* is one of the great revelations of His nature in the Hebrew Bible.

*v. 8 "pupils of Your own eyes" can also be translated "the apple of the eye", a figurative expression for something a person delights in. We can see this expression more literally (guard me as carefully as You would protect Your own pupils—though we know God does not have physical eyes) or more figuratively (protect me as the apple of Your eye=the one You delight in), either way the phrase shows how valued the pray-er sees their own worth in God's sight.

18 Victory

It feels good to win. It is a great feelings to throw our hands up in the air in victory. It's even better when that triumph comes after what seemed like certain defeat. If we are snatched from death and overwhelming odds and given victory by God, how much more there is to celebrate!

Psalm 18 is the longest psalm we have come across yet (but not the longest in the whole collection – that would be Psalm 119). Even so, its fifty verses can be read slowly in less than four minutes. The prayer arises from David's experience of deliverance from his enemies and even from Saul who had pursued him. Read all the way through Psalm 18 now in your own Bible.

God Gives Victory

Isn't this an elaborate song of victory? It's much more than, "God, You delivered me. I have won over my enemies. Great is the victory You have given me!"

Focus on the first three verses:

1) I love You, Yahweh my strength!
2) Yahweh is my rocky crag, my mountain stronghold, my God and my rock—I seek safety and refuge in Him. He is my shield, my defender and my refuge.
3) I call on Yahweh, the one to be praised, and I am delivered from my enemies.

Those verses alone would make a good meditation. God is my rock, He is my safe place of protection. God shields and covers me. All I have to do is call on Him. Zoom! He's there for me.

But there's much more inside this prayer. In several longer sections, David draws on elaborate poetry and military language to show what God has done.

The Epic Deliverer. With death wrapping its ropes around David, dragging him down to the deep, he calls on God in distress and is saved. Then in epic scale and dramatic thunder, Yahweh's deliverance is described so that David is brought out of the whirlpool waters(vv. 7-19).and put in a wide open safe place.

The Righteous God. Why does God do this? Because His nature is righteous and He will turn over heaven and earth to save the righteous and be a refuge to them (vv. 20-30).

Supreme General. Though David was trained to raise sheep and had no warlike spirit or military ambition, God chose him as king of Israel and he faced many enemies who were determined to fight and crush him. Even as a soldier, David did not boast in his battle skills. He knew God was the source of his strength (vv. 31-45).

46) Yahweh lives! Blessed is my Rock! High and exalted be God, my salvation,
47) the God who avenges me and subdued peoples under me,
48) who rescued me from my enemies and lifted me above those who oppose me, saving me from the violent.

49) For all this I sing Your praise to the nations; Yahweh, I sing to Your name and fame.
50) Great victories He gives to His king and He shows steadfast love to His anointed, to David and his descendants forever.

David had great reason to praise God for his victory. Do you also have a victory you should raise to God? Where are you feeling pressed and maybe even distressed to give up on God's promises? Don't let death kill your hope in God. Instead, claim the victory by calling on God in humility. He will train you for victory and deliver you as He has so many others.

Pray: God, victory is in Your name. Rescue me, deliver me from _____. Be my high Rock and mountain Refuge where I find safety and protection. I will not shake in fear; I will call on You in confidence. God, thank You in advance for Your victory in _____. Amen!

Write out the first three verses in your journal and meditate on them today.

Other Psalms like this: Psalm 62

19 God's Law

What is true? How do we know it is true? These are common questions that we all ask at times in our life. They are appropriate too, because there is a lot of untruth and many lies that pose as the truth.

We can certainly pray to God, "Show me the truth. Make clear to me what is real and true." We should also pay attention and see that God has already made a great deal of truth obvious to us.

Look at creation. From the heavens to the expanse of earth, there are many things to learn about what is true. The sun is one good example. Though you cannot look directly at it, without the sun and its light you wouldn't be able to see anything. You would be stumbling around in the dark.

But look also into God's Word. He has made His will known and revealed important truths about our hearts, our choices and how we should behave. Read and pray over the following psalm.

1) The heavens declare the glory of God, the expanse of sky proclaims what His hands have made.
2) Day after day pours forth new words and night after night brings forth knowledge;
3) yet there is no speaking and no words and no sound from all this silent testimony.
4) Their message goes out over the whole earth and to the extremes of the world.

God made a place in the sky for the sun 5) which is like a joyful bridegroom coming out of his wedding chamber or like a confident strong man ready to run his race.
6) Rising at one end of the sky and running its course to the other end, there is nothing that can be hidden from its glow.

7) The teaching* (*torah*) of Yahweh is perfect, it gives new life and strength.
The testimonies* of Yahweh can be trusted and give wisdom to the untrained and inexperienced.
8) The instructions* of Yahweh are right and straight, bringing joy to the heart.
The commands* of Yahweh are clean and pure, they make the eyes light up.
9) The fear of Yahweh** is good and pure, it will last forever.
The judgments* of Yahweh are true, and they are always fair and "just right."
10) I desire Your law and word much more than great amounts of the purest refined gold.
They are sweeter than honey, the purest honey straight from the comb.
11) I your servant am warned and instructed by Your commands, and in obeying them I am rewarded greatly.
12) Who can see and understand his own errors? No one can—free me from my hidden faults!
13) Keep me safe also from willful sins I know are wrong; don't let them make me their slave.
Then I will be blameless before You and free from serious sin.
14) I pray that my words spoken and what I meditate on in my mind and heart are pleasing to You.
Yahweh, You are my rock of protection and the One who rescues and redeems me from sin.

This psalm tells us that God has done much to reveal Himself, both through the world and through His word. The most important things God has said are not facts about the world but truths about how to live and how to put our lives on the right path.

The sun is a fitting example. It gives bright light to us. Likewise, God's word provides light for our path. Some people in the past have worshipped the sun as a god, but God's law has taught us this is wrong. There are other sins we commit that God teaches us to distinguish and avoid. Some of our sins are "hidden" from us, we are unaware of them and how they distort things. But God can free us from them, so we pray for our release.

There are also bad choices we make even though we know they are wrong. We also need rescue from these sins so they don't dominate us.

God can do all of this and more. We turn our hearts to Him and give Him our worship. His thoughts are more precious to us than anything else on earth.

What part of this prayer has shown you a new insight or truth? Have you put God as your highest desire and greatest reward (vv. 10-11)? Write out the verses from this psalm that have spoken most powerfully to you today. Memorize verse 14.

Other Psalms like this: Psalm 119

*teaching (*torah*) vv. 7-9 uses five different words for God's law, but all of them are related. *Torah* can mean teaching, instruction or law. We saw it first in Psalm 1. Interestingly, there are five books at the beginning of the Bible called the Torah or Law of Moses.
*testimonies (*edoth*) v. 7 a witness or testimony, **reminder of God's truth**
*instructions (*piqqud*) v. 8 instruction, procedure, precept, **how to do what is right**
*commands (*mitzvah*) v. 8 commandment, **what God wants and expects of us**

*judgments (*mishpat*) v. 9 a legal requirement or a judgment given, **what God's law requires**

**fear of Yahweh (*yirath Yahweh*) v. 9 – this could be the same as the fear of God mentioned in Psalm 15:4 and elsewhere in the Wisdom books (Proverbs, Ecclesiastes, Job, some Psalms). It *could* also be an expression for God's law, such as "the proper reverence and honor given to God", though this would be unusual. It seems to prepare us for what follows in vv. 10-11 and the rest of the psalm.

20 Your Name

When was the last time someone made fun of your name? How did you feel about it?

Sometimes we make fun of a name if we are close to someone or we even make up a nickname to show we are close. But usually we make fun of someone because we are being mean or it's a way to annoy them.

To make fun of someone's name is one way to disrespect them. That's why we don't like people doing it to us. What about the opposite? Can you show respect for someone's name? When I lived in China people asked me what my last name was by saying, "What is your honored surname?" In fact, it is a common expression in Chinese.

To treat someone's name with respect and honor or to disrespect and cut them down—this shows what we think of them. And to take up the name of God in prayer is to show that we respect God, honor Him and expect great things from heaven. Look at how Psalm 20 begins.

1) May Yahweh answer you in the time of trouble. May the name of Jacob's God protect you!
2) May He send you help from His holy place and support you from Zion.

Help, support, and answered prayer are coming from God. Pray with faith and expectancy. You are not alone in this. The tempo is rising.

4) May He give you your heart's desire and make all your plans succeed.

5) Let us raise a shout over your victory and lift banners in the name of God.
May Yahweh fulfill all your requests.

As we pray, we start celebrating the victory God has given us. Like an army on the march we raise our flags that show who we honor—it's God. We trust in God's name to protect us and win the day.

6) Now I know that God gives victory to His anointed king, He answers him from His holy heaven with miraculous deeds of deliverance by His great power.
7) Some trust in chariots, some trust in warhorses, but we call upon the name of Yahweh our God.

The chariots and warhorses were fearsome weapons of war in the ancient world (see Isaiah 31:1, 3), and Israel was tempted to call on Egypt for help and trust in what we call "superior firepower". Today, we trust in money, wealth, science and technology to carry us through. This prayer urges us to rightly call on the powerful name of God—*that* is where true help is found.

Prayer: God, I honor Your name. You are holy and mighty. Help is found in You alone. Lord, my heart's desire is _____ . Today I ask you to make my plans succeed. I raise a shout of victory to You and celebrate Your great name. Hallelu-Yah! Praise God!

Other Psalms like this: Psalm 138, 46

21 Answered

When we pray for something we are looking for an answer. When you pray, do you expect an answer? When you get an answer, what do you do next?

In Psalm 20 there was such a strong expectation that God would answer that prayer and give all that was sought and desired. The confidence placed in God's name and honor, that He would come through, was hard to miss.

Psalm 21 sounds like part 2 of that prayer, only now the dominant note is rejoicing and celebration at God's answer to the king's prayer.

1) Yahweh, the king rejoices in Your strength and might, and in your victory* what tremendous praise he gives up!
2) You have given him his heart's desire and have not held back what he requested.
3) For You meet him with rich blessings and set a crown of pure gold on his head.
4) He asked you for life and You gave it to him—a long life stretching on and on.
5) His glory is great through Your help*; splendor and majesty You give to him.
6) You give him blessings forever; You make him glad with the joy of Your presence.
7) For the king trusts in Yahweh, and through the steadfast love of the Most High the king will not be shaken.

Is it hard for you to pray a prayer that features a king? Almost no one reading this is a king—or even distantly related to royalty. Yet, there are a number of psalms written by the king or about the king in the collection of 150 psalms in our Bible. What do we do with those?

First, what God has done for the king, He has in fact done for His entire people. The king represents all of us. You don't have to be a king to relate with what these prayers say.

Also, the king represents something we aspire to. The king has special favor and blessing, and we desire that closeness to God in our own praying. We approach God and have no disadvantage to a king—God hears us the same.

Finally, a king has a broader perspective—and a wider responsibility— than ordinary people. If you were to pray as a king, you would probably be asking for more than individual concerns and small favors. You would pray for salvation for an entire nation or blessing that is great enough to spread around generously.

How has God answered your prayers? How are you rejoicing and celebrating His goodness? Are you praying to Him like a king and asking for greater things than just your personal benefits? This psalm teaches us: pray like a king!

The final part of the psalm sees an end to the king's enemies— Yahweh will do them in. Their plans and plots will not succeed. This echoes Psalm 2. The prayer ends on a final word that turns toward God.

13) Be exalted, Yahweh, in Your strength. We will sing praises to Your power.

Prayer: God, You are strong and mighty. You give me strength and I rejoice in Your mighty deliverance. God, You have answered my prayers for _____ and _____. You expand my vision and give me confidence to ask for even more like a king, not for myself but for Your purposes and so Your will is done. I praise You God!

Other Psalms like this: Psalm 2, 72, 110, 45

*victory (v. 1), help (v. 5) are the same word in Hebrew (*yeshuah*), and the same word is used in Psalm 20:5. It can be translated as victory or help. It emphasizes that victory or help come from God.

22 Lonely Cry of Lament

Today's prayer may take a little longer, especially when you read the extra verses from Mark or Matthew, but it will be worth it.

Many prayers in the Psalms are laments—they have a sad note to them and strong emotions. They show us we can bring our strongest feelings to God and they teach us just how to do that. We find more laments early in Psalms and more praise in the later psalms. There is probably some wisdom in this arrangement.

The life of faith—truly believing in God each day, is sometimes compared to a roller coaster ride with ups and downs. This psalm uses a different metaphor. It's more like walking along in life and then falling into a seeming bottomless pit and feeling utterly forsaken and unheard there even as you struggle to believe God will come through.

1) My God, My God, why have You left me here alone? Why so far from saving me and my screaming for help?
2) O God, I cry to You by day—You don't answer. At night I cry and I get no peace nor rest—just silence.
3) But *You*—Holy One—sit on a throne, the One whom Israel praises.
4) Our fathers trusted in *You*. They trusted, and You rescued them.
5) They cried out and they escaped by Your help, they trusted You and were not shamed or disappointed.

6) But I am a worm, not a man. I am reviled by men and despised by the people.
7) Everyone who sees me mocks me; they taunt and make fun of me.

8) "Rely on Yahweh to take away your troubles," they mock. "Let Him save you."

"He will deliver you because He sure likes you-hah!"

9) You were at my birth, seeing that I safely entered the world, and You were with me through my early years.

10) My fate depended on You from the day I was born, and all along You have been my God.

11) Do not be far from me for trouble is near and there is no one to help me.

It goes on, comparing the troubles to attacks by wild animals and to a wasting illness that ravages the body. (vv. 12-18)

19) But You, Yahweh, don't stay far away. My strength, hurry and help me!

21) Deliver me from the lion's mouth; from the horns of wild bulls—You hear me!

22) I will tell the brothers near of what Your name has done. I will praise You in the assembly of God's people.

23) You who fear Yahweh, praise Him! Jacob's descendants, glorify Him! Stand awestruck before Him, all you descendants of Israel!

24) He did not ignore or scorn , He did not detest the suffering of the lowly. He did not hide His face from him, but when he cried for help, God heard and answered.

25) From You comes my praise in the great congregation; I pay my vows in the presence of those who worship and fear You.

In fact, God *does* come through and the praise and celebration that follows takes us up to the mountain peaks and out of the pit. Everything in the last third of the psalm is praise; all notes of lament are gone. The praise starts with the one who was suffering and is expressed concretely in acts of worship (v. 25). It includes the people of God but expands outward to include the whole earth and reaches from the rich and mighty down to those in the grave, even stretching through the generations before and those yet to come.

The prayer ends on an emphatic note: God *has acted* righteously in delivering His people.

This prayer has a strong link to the life and death of Jesus. Go read either Mark 15:16-34 or Matthew 27:27-46 now. Don't miss this—you will be amazed! Not only did Jesus heal and comfort the suffering during his ministry on earth, he himself prayed this very prayer while suffering on the cross. He later rose to life and then rose from the mountain up to heaven after defeating death and being delivered from the grave.

How do *you* pray this prayer? Have you experienced the extreme loneliness of feeling God has left you and is far, far away? Have you felt as if you were left to die alone without anyone caring at all? If so, you can take up this prayer.

How about if you have not had that extreme experience of aloneness or death breathing down your neck? The truth is, God has entered into that pit and embraced that exact experience for us. Regardless of our feelings, we do not suffer alone because God is there. And He does not leave us there alone and abandoned. He lifts us up and delivers us.

This is an amazing truth. Write out the following prayer slowly in your journal and let the words penetrate your soul.

Prayer: My God, My God, why have You left me here alone? Why so far from saving me and my screaming for help? O God, I cry to You by day—You don't answer. At night I cry and I get no peace nor rest—just silence. This feels awful. How could you allow it? Do not be far from me for trouble is near and there is no one to help me. And yet, when the night is darkest, You are there. You come through and deliverance is surely coming. I lift up praise to You, because You know my suffering and even worse that I cannot imagine. But Your presence is here with me and Your triumph is sure. Praise be to God!

Other Psalms like this: Psalm 30, 6

23 Shepherd and Host

Psalm 23 is probably the best known and loved prayer in the entire collection. It is familiar, comforting, quotable. We will use it to lead us in prayer, to teach us the next thing we need to know about growing closer to God.

1) Yahweh is my shepherd, so I have everything I need.
2) He lets me rest in green pastures, He leads me to quiet pools of water
3) He revives new life in me, he leads me down the right paths that are safe and good because His name is honorable.
4) Even if I walk through deepest darkness, I am not afraid of harm or evil, for You are with me.
   Your rod (cudgel) and shepherd's staff protect me.
5) As a Host, you prepare a rich feast and set it out before me; it's plain to my enemies You protect me.
   You welcome me as an honored guest pouring olive oil on my head and fill my cup generously.
6) For certain your goodness and steadfast love will be with me my whole life, and I will keep returning to Yahweh's house as long as I live.

It is easy to picture this psalm coming from David and his own life experience. His early training was as a shepherd, and as a young man who had to run from King Saul he knew the difference between a good and bad host. For a better understanding of this background, read 1 Samuel 17:34-37 (shepherd); 1 Samuel 22:3-4; 25:1-39 (host).

David highlights the provision and protection that God gives as Shepherd and Host. He also emphasizes another truth about us that we might easily miss. We are not long on this earth nor permanent residents. We are nomadic like sheep, travelers without permanent homes. That truth is the reason we need a good Shepherd, a gracious Host.

This prayer of trust and faith helps us tell the truth about ourselves and to look to God as the one we truly should hope in.

Pray: Go back and read over the psalm again and pray all six verses slowly. Which line or verse especially speaks to you right now? Write that one out in your journal. What specific way does this prayer connect with your life right now? Include that in your journal as well.

Other Psalms like this: Psalm 100, 28, 16

24 Worship Ready

Are you ready to worship? How do we enter God's presence?
Whether you are going to church, a prayer meeting, small group or a
worship service, use this prayer to train you to enter into worship.

You can think of worship as intensified prayer, a meeting with God.
This psalm was probably used to celebrate the ark of the covenant in
ancient Israel being brought to the place of worship.*   It has
continued to speak to and for God's people to help them enter more
fully into the right worship of God.

1) The earth and everything in it belong to Yahweh, the world and
all that lives in it are His.
2) He brought it forth from the deep seas and established it on the
great currents.
3) Who can ascend the mountain of Yahweh to worship Him? Who
can go up to His holy temple?
4) The one free from guilty hands and who has a pure heart, who
does not worship idols nor swears falsely.
5) They will receive Yahweh's rich blessing; God saves and makes
them righteous.
6) These are the kind of people who seek and approach God, who
seek the presence of the God of Jacob.
7) Open wide the gates, swing open the ancient city doors, so the
King of glory may enter.
8) Who is this King of glory? Yahweh, strong and mighty; Yahweh,
mighty in winning wars.
9) Open wide the gates, swing open the ancient city doors, so the
King of glory may enter.
10) Who is He, this King of glory? Yahweh Leader of warriors, He
is the King of glory!

Three points, briefly.

First, it all starts with God. He created the world. Everything belongs to Him. He started everything, long before we came around. Let's keep everything in the right perspective: God first, we just got here.

Second, what are you seeking? Are you pursuing a feeling or emotion, perhaps holiness, or a "high" or happiness? You may—or may not—find that in worship. What you *should* be seeking is God and His presence. To do so, come clean. Is there any sin or guilt that is going to get in the way? Deal with it—now. Confess it and ask God for forgiveness. Once you have done that, climb the mountain. Enter in and don't hang back. Don't let your feelings or any condemnation hold you back. God blesses, He saves and He makes us righteous.

Third, put yourself into it fully. Open wide those gates, let the King enter in. The battle is won, let Him have His way. He will make His glory shine in you if you are willing. Open the door wider still.

This prayer draws us back again to the first verse. Repeat it, memorize it, meditate on it. The whole world belongs to God. Prepare your heart to worship Him. Open the gates of your heart wide and let Him in.

Other Psalms like this: Psalm 100, 118

*For the fuller background about this, look at 1 Samuel 4:3,10-11, 7:1, 2 Samuel 6:12-18, 1 Kings 8:1-6. In the days of Samuel the ark was captured by the Philistines but then later returned to Israel. David in his time brought the ark into the gates of Jerusalem to the part called the City of David. Solomon in his reign built the temple and brought the ark up from the City of David onto the temple mount where it was placed in the temple.

25 Waiting

Who likes to wait? Most of us don't. It seems like a waste of time or an insult ("who does she think she is, making me wait?"). It can feel like we are stuck in between activities or awaiting a decision.

I grew up in New Mexico, and I recall a time almost twenty years ago when I was in Albuquerque and needed help with my car. A kind man gave me a ride and we discussed waiting. Living among the Pueblo Indians, this man had learned that waiting is a very human activity just like eating, reading, or farming, and not just a boring, pointless waste of time, "doing nothing."

One important lesson to learn in prayer is to wait on the Lord. It is an activity in its own right. Psalms of lament are the most common type in the collection of *Psalms*, and lament is really about waiting. Answers can come swiftly, but they also can come after a time of waiting. Psalm 25 teaches us about waiting. Read the entire Psalm from your own Bible or a new version before going further.

There are three themes that surface in this psalm. They are trust, being taught the truth, and forgiveness of sins. We have encountered each of them already in the earlier psalms (1-24), but they can all be found here in this one prayer.

1) Yahweh, I desire You. 2) My God, in You I trust. Don't let me be shamed or let my enemies rejoice at my expense!
3) All who wait for You—they will not be ashamed. They will be shamed who betray others without reason.

4) Yahweh, I want to know your paths; teach me your ways.
5) Guide me in your true way and teach me, for You are God, my deliverer. It is You I look to and turn to all day long.

6) Remember, O Yahweh, Your compassion and steadfast love,
   that's always Who you've been.
7) Don't recall though the sins of my youth and my other wrongs;
   remember instead *Your* steadfast love for me—it's because of
   Your goodness Yahweh!

We live in an instant society. Impatience is all around us—and in us. Trust requires us to wait. Learning God's truth and really taking it into us requires time. Forgiveness teaches us also to wait on God rather than trying to do enough good to "earn" His forgiveness (it will never work anyway). When we forgive others we also learn to become like God and to wait on Him, not to rush to judgment or to take revenge ourself.

This psalm is rich and can be prayed many times with different points to emphasize and learn from. Focus on one verse or line from the psalm that especially speaks to You. Repeat it and take its truth into your soul. Which line or word is it? Does it speak of trust, learning God's truth, forgiveness, or another spiritual truth? Write that in your journal and return to this psalm as you walk and grow with God.

26 Walk in Integrity

We all have been misunderstood. Have you felt wrongly accused? It could be a small mistake or a very serious charge brought against you. How do you pray through such an experience? Turn to Psalm 26 and read through it (12 verses).

Psalm 26 provides a key for us. It is repeated twice, at the beginning and the end of the psalm (vv. 1 and 11). The key phrase (in Hebrew) is this: "I walk in my integrity." Most English translations have something about living blameless. When we are misunderstood or accused wrongly, even more important than mounting a vigorous defense, *walk in integrity*. Rather than being pulled down into discouragement, live in innocence and purity.

Can you pray that? "I walk in my integrity."

There are two different attitudes possible when we are wrongly accused. One is justifying ourselves: "I am good, I know it and I'll prove it." It is confidence in our own goodness. The other is pleading to God: "No matter how innocent I am of the false charges, I'm putting my full hope in You, God, Your   goodness and fairness." This is faith in God's goodness and power to set things right.

When you read Psalm 26, it may sound like the first attitude is present: "I have led a blameless life...I don't sit with the deceitful...or hyprocrites...evildoers...the wicked. I am innocent and I love the house of God."

In truth, though, this is a prayer to God based on need. The charge against the one praying may be serious and deliverance is really needed. This prayer is not the boast or brag of someone confident in their own spirituality or rightness.

What do we learn about how to pray from this psalm? When we are misunderstood or wrongly charged with something we didn't do, the human tendency is to protest our innocence, to feel hurt, to focus on ourselves. This psalm trains us to focus instead on God. Invite Him in, let Him come close and examine our heart. Walk in His truth. Rest in His faithful love.

Worship God and join with others who are likewise focused on God. Don't ask advice from those who are not close friends of God. Avoid spending time around people who are two-faced or who don't tell the truth about themselves or God.

This is what it means to walk in integrity. Make it your prayer today.

Prayer: God, I'm setting my eye on Your steadfast love. I'm going to walk in Your true paths. Anything else lacks integrity and cannot hold up. God, I walk in my integrity. I walk in You.

27 Confidence

The psalms teach us how to pray, especially when we are in some very difficult situations. Doubt, discouragement, sickness, enemies, being abandoned, being falsely accused, even the threat of death—these are desperate places to be. We learn to pray even—and especially—in these tough times.

At these times you might feel crushed or barely able to hold on, maybe even like you are slipping away. There's another possibility in our prayer. Such difficulties can actually strengthen our faith and help us to rise up in confidence. Consider Psalm 27.

1) Yahweh is my light and my salvation, whom will I fear? Like a fortress Yahweh guards my life, whom will I dread?
3) Even if a whole army sets up camp around me, my heart will not fear. If war breaks out against me, I will have confidence in God.
4) I have asked Yahweh for one thing, and this is what I really want: to live in Yahweh's house all my life, to gaze on Yahweh's beauty, to ask for guidance in his temple.
5) In times of trouble he will hide me in His shelter, tuck me away in His tent, put me up safe and high on a rock no one can reach.
6) No hanging my head! I'm raising it in triumph over my enemies. I will offer sacrifices with shouts of joy in God's place. I will make praise and sing to Yahweh!

The notes of confidence are strong. It is uplifting to read this prayer. It actually pulls you in and elevates your spirit to join in this confident faith.

Don't be mistaken. This is not just heightened feeling or summoning up some courage for ourselves. This is about focusing like a laser beam on just one thing: God.

7) Hear me, Yahweh, when I call to You. Show me Your favor and answer me.
8) The command to seek Your presence, to worship You, has reached my heart. I'm seeking Your face, Yahweh!
9) Don't hide Your face from me and don't cast me aside in anger; You have been my help!
Don't abandon me and don't leave me; You are the God of my salvation!
10) Even if my father and mother abandon me, Yahweh will take me in and care for me.

The key point is: Will you turn to God and seek Him no matter what? Will you hold to Him over all opposition (including your own parents), even if your own feelings betray you and you think God is angry at you or abandoning you? If you are not sure, not confident of God, make that your prayer. "God, show me your unstoppable love. Reveal to me how far You are willing to go for me."

11) Teach me Your way (derek), Yahweh, and lead me along an even, safe path because stalkers are watching me.
12) Don't give me up to the will of my enemies, for they rise up against me as lying witnesses to falsely accuse me with threats of violence.
13) I believe beyond a doubt I will live to see Yahweh's goodness before I die, here and now.
14) Put your trust in Yahweh. Be confident in your heart, because you put your trust in Yahweh!

Confidence is not summoning up something within ourselves. It is an act of putting full faith in God. Which line speaks most clearly to your heart? Put your confidence in God as you pray those words and make them your own.

More Psalms like this: Psalm 23, 18, 16, 91

28 He Hears

If you were absolutely certain that God hears every word, every prayer you pray, how would that change the way you pray?

Think about it a minute. Would you pray for more *stuff*? Would you pray to be a *better person*? Would you ask for a *miracle*? Learn from Psalm 28 about praying in assurance that He hears.

1) O Yahweh, to You I call, do not be deaf to me.
   Unless You respond to me I will be like those who go down to the pit of death.
2) Listen to the sound of my plea for mercy, my cry for help to You.
   I lift my hands to the holiest place in Your temple.

Direct. This is the key to prayer that is heard. Be direct and pray from the heart.

Take it direct, go to God and seek His face, His holy presence.

It's not dependent on how well we pray or the technique we use. It is God's mercy we depend on. He hears because that is who He is, a merciful God.

6) Blessed be Yahweh, for He has heard the sound of my plea for mercy.
7) Yahweh is my strength and my shield; my heart trusts in Him and I am helped.
   I am thrilled and rejoicing; I glorify Him with my song.
8) Yahweh is the strength of His people; He is a stronghold for the deliverance of His anointed.
9) Save your people and bless your heritage; be their shepherd and carry them forever.

This is the truth: He hears. Pray believing that He hears, because God delights in showing us mercy. It is His own nature. We are His people. You are His child. He will show you favor.

Prayer: Today's prayer is to go back through the psalm and pray it yourself, slowly and deliberately. Make the sound of pleading for mercy and be specific about where you sense the need for mercy. Confess it to God. He will hear it, and He will change You if You plead for his favor.

29 Voice of God

How do you feel about thunderstorms? When towering clouds darken and lightning flashes followed by thunder claps and howling winds—are you scared, excited, or maybe both?

Today's psalm shows us how to pray in the middle of mighty forces of nature, and it reminds us that behind and above the storm, there is a God even greater, more powerful, and deserving of our praise.

1) Ascribe to Yahweh, you heavenly beings,
   Ascribe to Yahweh glory and strength
2) Ascribe to Yahweh the glory of His name,
   Worship Yahweh, majestic in holiness.
3) The voice* of Yahweh is over the waters;
   The God of glory thunders,
   Yahweh is over the mighty waters.
4) The voice of Yahweh is power;
   The voice of Yahweh is majesty,
5) The voice of Yahweh breaks the cedar trees,
      Yahweh shatters the cedars of Lebanon.
6) He makes Lebanon skip like a calf,
   and Sirion like a young wild ox.
7) The voice of Yahweh flashes flames of fire.
8) The voice of Yahweh makes the wilderness tremble,
   Yahweh makes the wilderness of Kadesh tremble.
9) The voice of Yahweh causes the deer to give birth (*or* the oaks to
   twist) and strips the forest bare,
   in His temple all say, "Glory!"
10) Yahweh sat enthroned over the Flood*,
    Yahweh sits enthroned, King forever.
11) May Yahweh give strength to His people,
    May Yahweh bless His people with peace and wellbeing.

How do you like the rhythm and raw power of this prayer? The words are poetry, but the sound is clearly...the voice of Yahweh!

Our prayers do not have to be poetic or a bunch of beautiful words in order to be heard. But *can* we use poetry, rhythm and moving words to pray to God if we are inclined that way? Psalm 29 (and others) say certainly we can.

There is something else. This psalm proclaims Yahweh's glory not just in the fury of the storm, but it places God's power supreme to chaos, it traces the source of God's power back to His holiness, it arouses praise by acknowledging God's glory.

In this psalm we learn to pray using poetry and by listening to the voice of God. In our response we lift God up to His rightful place: over the storm, high and holy, enthroned in glory as we praise Him. What a mighty God we serve!

Prayer: Go back and read through the psalm again out loud. Let God's powerful voice speak to you today and obey whatever He might tell you to do. Write this in your journal.

Other Psalms like this: Psalm 96

*voice in vv. 3,4,5,7,8,9 *qol* ("voice, sound") The *qol Yahweh* ("voice of Yahweh"), repeated 7 times, is powerful, epic, active, and effective. Another meaning of Yahweh's voice is "thunder" (see the parallel in v. 3). Emphasis is on the power of His voice more than what He says.
*flood in v. 10 *mabbul* ("flood"), the only other place this word is used is in Genesis 6-9 in the story of the Flood. This psalm shows God in control over the mighty flood and the forces of destruction that it unleashes.

30 Mourning to Morning

Reversal. That's when things get turned around—completely. The day starts great...and then something happens and it starts to fall apart. It gets bad, couldn't get worse. Until it does. That's a reversal from good to bad.

Of course lament and weeping are appropriate then. It may be the *only* kind of prayer you can manage if you even remember to do that.

Will it never get better? It seems hopeless. But reversal can work the other way. From the dark, slimy pit of despair you can be lifted out into the light. From deep sadness you can discover a lifting sense of joy. Reversal—it can happen with God.

1) I exalt [lift high] Yahweh, for You have lifted me up and You did not let my enemies rejoice over me!
2) Yahweh my God, I cried out to You for help, and You healed me.
3) Yahweh You brought up my soul from *Sheol**, You restored my life from going down to the Pit of death.*

4) Sing and make music to Yahweh you godly people, praise and recall all His holiness and holy acts,
5) For His anger lasts only a moment but when He is pleased there is lasting life;
   Weeping comes for the night, but cries of rejoicing and shouts of joy come with the morning!

That is a reversal indeed! From near death to God's healing and deliverance; from sadness, sobbing and weeping comes God's favor, His pleasure and the shouts of joy that it brings.

The whole cycle gets replayed, repeated again in the second half of the psalm, but with a little more detail. So we learn this: Prayer is a time to meditate, to ponder, to replay God's goodness and His acts of kindness that deliver us from great difficulty. Join in the prayer as you meditate on these words.

6) I said, in my time of ease and comfort, "I won't be shaken or moved—ever!"
7) Yahweh, in Your favor and pleasure You made me as firm as a mighty mountain.
[But suddenly] You hid your face and I was terrified.
8) To You I called "Yahweh!", to my Lord God I begged for compassion.
9) What do You gain from my death, from me going down in the Pit? Will the dust praise You? Can it tell of Your faithfulness?
10) Hear Yahweh, and show grace and favor to me! Yahweh be my help!

11) You did it! You turned my sad wailing into dancing; You took off my mourning clothes and clothed me with joy and gladness
12) so that with my best I may sing your praise and not be silent. O Yahweh my God, forever I will praise You!

Did you notice the reversal at the beginning of this part? God's grace and blessing was turned into selfish boasting and pride. We easily see prosperity and blessing as a sign of God's favor. But withdrawing it from us so we can deal with a deadly heart problem, which is what pride is, also shows us God's grace and kindness. When God's presence has gone, it is a signal that something has gone wrong and we need to take it as a warning.

The return to favor begins with us seeing how dangerous the situation is and admitting it. "God! I did wrong and I need your help." And sure as the sun rises, God is there turning weeping and mourning into

a morning of joy and gladness, praise and blessing. Surrender yourself to His grace and goodness!
You have turned my mourning-lament into dancing (v. 12)

Prayer: Verses 5 and 11 are memorable. Write them out in your journal. Meditate on their truth.
Pray either verse 10 or the last part of verse 12 depending on which one fits your situation now:
"Hear Yahweh, and show grace and favor to me! Yahweh be my help!"
"O Yahweh my God, forever I will praise You!"

Other Psalms like this: Psalm 6, 22, 34, 116

*v.3 *Sheol* – see notes on Psalms 6, 16
*v.3 *Pit of death* (bor-world of the dead; pit). Hebrew poetry often puts two similar words together to give a fuller sense. Sheol and the Pit of death represent the same thing with two different words to describe this awful experience that seemed near to death.

Keep Praying

Now that you have spent a month praying through the first thirty psalms, what do you do next?

Keep praying of course!

The power of using the Psalms is that it guides and launches our prayers. The Psalms take us deeper and further than we would usually go on our own. That's one of the reasons God's people have kept using them over thousands of years.

You can do this several ways. One is to get a Bible (the one you use already or a new one) and read a psalm every day and commit to praying it. I have found using a new translation can open up new avenues of prayer. Some translations or versions of the Bible are poetic, some are more literal, others aim to communicate the same meaning and impact as the original Hebrew without being "word for word" or what we call "wooden".

Some of the longer psalms might need to be broken down or covered over several days. We have seen many types of psalms in this book, but we haven't encountered all of them. There are more royal psalms, worship hymns, narrative or storytelling psalms than we have been able to share.

You can also look for other books in this series of praying through the psalms – *God Help Me Grow*.

You have already accomplished something positive in your walk with God by praying through 30 psalms. Continue down this path and ask God, "Help me grow, please."

I pray you have been encouraged and built up. Let me hear from you and share your experience of praying through the psalms.

Baruch Shemo! (Bless His name)
Ron